# BRIMSTONE

# BRIMSTONE
## a book of villanelles

### John Kinsella

PUBLICATIONS

2020

Published by Arc Publications,
Nanholme Mill, Shaw Wood Road
Todmorden OL14 6DA, UK
www.arcpublications.co.uk

978 1908376 09 1 (pbk)
978 1910345 09 2 (ebk)


Design by Tony Ward
Printed in Great Britain by TJ International Ltd,
Padstow, Cornwall

ACKNOWLEDGEMENTS

Some of these poems previously appeared
in the following journals:
*Australian Academies of Humanities, Australian Book Review, Cordite,
Crikey, Fiddlehead, Kenyon Review* online, *Meanjin,
Mutually Said* blog, *Plume, Southern Review,
Times Literary Supplement.*

A few of the earlier villanelles were published in my books
*The Silo: A Pastoral Symphony, The New Arcadia,
The Jaguar's Dream,* and *A Shared Wonder of Light: poems and
photographs from West Cork* (with photographer John D'Alton).

Thanks to Curtin University and
Churchill College, Cambridge University.
Thanks to family, as always.

Supported using public funding by
ARTS COUNCIL
ENGLAND
LOTTERY FUNDED

**Arc International Poets
Series Editor: James Byrne**

# CONTENTS

## DEDICATION: BRIMSTONE BUTTERFLIES

*for Tim Cribb on his 80th*


The fens are a place of work but also theatre,
and where we follow the Cam to Grantchester
pause while brimstone butterflies gather.

Even over the decades we have known each other,
the cow parsley has changed its speech, its manner,
the fens are a place of work but also theatre.

And seasons undoing seasons are the director's
challenge but one through which each of us is an actor,
and we all pause while brimstone butterflies gather.

It's March and insect-time as the calendar
gathers on itself to keep things in kilter,
the fens are a place of work but also theatre.

For you, Tim, the theatre is a fen tiger
that is a mask behind a mask and it's May and a darter
needs an understudy as brimstone butterflies can't gather.

When strife and revelry stretch 'night' to 'aurora'
we throw aside conventions and shout 'Honour'!
The fens are a place of work but also theatre,
so pause while brimstone butterflies gather.

Jean Passerat
**VILLANELLE**


My turtledove is lost:
But isn't it she who calls?
I want to follow her flight.

You are missing your mate,
Alas! I miss mine as well,
My turtledove is lost.

My faith is as fast,
As your love faithful,
I want to follow her flight.

You renew your plaints;
And I must lament as well:
My turtledove is lost.

Since the beauty is absent
I no longer see anything beautiful:
I want to follow her flight.

Death whom I summon day and night
Take what's at your disposal:
My turtledove is lost,
I want to follow her flight.

*translated by John Kinsella*

## GOADING STORMS OUT OF A DARKENING FIELD

Goading storms out of a darkening field,
Cockeyed bobs seeding the salt, the farmer
Cursing the dry, cursing the bitter yield.

And while lightning would savage him with skilled
Thrusts, and floods strip the topsoil, it's better
Goading storms out of a darkening field

Than sit distraught on the verandah, killed
By the 'quitter's syndrome' – it's much safer
Cursing, the dry, cursing the bitter yield.

Field bins empty, coffers bare, should have sold
Two years back when prices were halfway there.
Goading storms out of a darkening field.

Red harvest, charred hills, dry wells filled and sealed.
Sheep on their last legs. Dams crusted over.
Cursing the dry, cursing the bitter yield.

It's tempting when prayers and patience have failed,
Diviners have lost track of ground water.
Goading storms out of a darkening field.
Cursing the dry, cursing the bitter yield.

## WHITE-FACED HERON

The white-faced heron seems grammar and action
as the sun sharpens poise and balance,
solitary in a field provokes a reaction.

Clots and twists of cloud confuse the fraction,
divisible quantity of math and trance,
the white-faced heron seems grammar and action.

The surety of her being creates an equation,
dawn and sunset trigger clairvoyance,
solitary in a field provokes a reaction.

We invest ourselves in her volatile station,
formulate moods on the fact of her presence,
the white-faced heron seems grammar and action.

It's the pattern of speech we define as tension,
the hope of her being there, the thrill of chance,
solitary in a field provokes a reaction.

Language shapes a waterbird's intention,
pasture and water shape her stance,
the white-faced heron seems grammar and action,
solitary in a field provokes a reaction.

## THE DAMAGE DONE

Someone is revving the shit out of a chainsaw;
We look up from flatlands to the wooded summit,
Up past the hillside paddocks, up at the place of law.

Policemen don't go there, it's not their law,
Whitegums cast no shade over sheep, roots of wattle vibrate,
Someone is revving the shit out of a chainsaw.

After the heatwave, vandals cut wood like straw,
The damage done out of sight, we hear them harvest into night,
Up past the hillside paddocks, up at the place of law.

Tomorrow, in extrovert morning light, it will be hard to ignore
Their lines of light, ghosts of the outcrop trapped in granite,
Someone is revving the shit out of a chainsaw.

Night birds stuck in raw, dark air, left to claw
Phantoms and microwaves, asides in the script,
Up past the hillside paddocks, up at the place of law.

Down here, the parrots have returned – there are more
Than we thought. They scan for seed out of habit.
Someone is revving the shit out of a chainsaw,
Up past the hillside paddocks, up at the place of law.

## AGAINST THE BURNINGS-OFF PATRIARCHY

Smoke columns lift from chaff fires
& survey remnant scrub that will burn, too,
a side-effect to expand the cropping area.

It's a year by year prospect, *the drier*
*the better* when torch is put to windrows,
and smoke columns lift from chaff fires.

What is our choking as a farmer
recovers that vision splendid – fighting the damned crows,
a side-effect to expand the cropping area?

What is denial as mushroom clouds reach higher
than denial, than roots of grandad's almanac, the *old* milieu,
as smoke columns lift from chaff fires?

All manners of control – *weeds & insects* – accrue
in the 'reasons for', the stubble-flamed echo
a side-effect to expand the cropping area.

And see the York gums burn to termite hollows
and see creek-scrub top-off and hear creatures call *to & fro*:
smoke columns lift from chaff fires,
a side-effect to expand the cropping area.

## THE PIONEERING CANOLA CROP

Pioneering signage of the yellow splash
where year by year a few more trees 'fall',
the GM canola crap and a crop is a rash.

Demi-edible photo-op to take the cash
crop crap a typo an error a patented hell,
pioneering signage of the yellow splash.

Who gets fed the rubbish of the new worlding dash
to the finish line as cooking fires are made grammatical
while the GM canola crap makes a crop a rash?

Misnomer is the hook that takes a chain a clash
of titans on the stock-market in the grainpool,
pioneering signage of the yellow splash.

These claims of holier-than-thou these shout-outs these calls
for worship because they 'feed us', as if *profit* is a by-line incidental –
the GM canola crap and a crop is a rash.

The servants of chemical companies of the brash
registered researchers tracking their glories their milestone miracles:
*pioneer*(ing) signage of the yellow splash –
the GM canola crap is crop with a rash.

## A GREEN LIMMAT RIVER: WITH GREAT SADNESS

The disconnect between cause and effect
as Uranine is poured into sharp contrast like snow melt,
the damaged river through the city is made bereft.

*Temporary...* as chemical warfare?... *temporary* as the best
laid plans floating in the bright emulsification of death – a test –
the disconnect between cause and effect.

Social media traces through screen memory through distinct
moments of play in the horror of on and on it goes left right left,
the damaged river through the city flows bereft.

Rebellion that feeds the extinction that synthesises and treats
'world' as playground to announce the leaks – halt!
the disconnect between cause and effect.

This landlocked calenture this old city called to order this cost
of confronting like a green algal bloom swallowing each breath,
the damaged river through the city is made bereft.

'As toxic as table salt' – sum of the parts – investigate the collect
& refining of salt, the world's hardening arteries, the logo the crest –
via this disconnect between cause and effect
the damaged river through the city flows bereft.

## 'WHOSE DISCORDANT SCREAMS WERE HEARD LONG BEFORE'

Thoreau ('Winter Animals')

*after the annual district 'fox-cull competition'*


Red fox on red firebreak emerges after the slaughter,
After the killings corellas hesitate in their flocking 'instinct',
Whose discordant screams were heard long before.

I make my outline against early morning, take a splinter
Of each shadow to ensure that all our fates are linked,
Red fox on red firebreak emerges after the slaughter.

Whether or not I believe, I agree that it strives to rain at Easter,
And apportion prayers to sky and ground and even blood – each distinct –
Whose discordant screams were heard long before.

It is said the fox that screams is never noisier
And that a flock of corellas is rarely silent,
Red fox on red firebreak emerges after the slaughter.

I have stories to go by, knowledge by which to enter,
But fear that outcomes are almost impossible to predict,
Whose discordant screams were heard long before.

Which is why through haze I see white as red, as colour,
And allow myself to be distracted by sunlight on a sun skink,
Red fox on red firebreak emerges after the slaughter,
Whose discordant screams were heard long before.

## DUROD

Green road cast in red rock
Was a conduit for copper
As Bird Island brewed kittiwakes.

Miners suspended on ropes, mattocks
Swinging to prise and not come a cropper –
Green road cast in red rock

When metal light escapes and shocks
A brazen sky, the dark glow of powder,
As Bird Island brewed kittiwakes.

Shims and quoins of cliff-face no stock-
Standard zone of worship, no screamer –
Green road cast in red rock.

Warding off those hostile flocks
They mistook a feather for copper,
As Bird Island brewed kittiwakes.

To undermine the face of a seasonal clock,
To rappel to the crux – the photographer's
Green road cast in red rock
As Bird Island brews kittiwakes.

## 'SHIP'S TIMBER'

We step into the reality of fiction,
The scene written that might be Brow Head –
Stone house left to the coast's contraction.

Levellers and random rubble, barely dressed stone,
The fireplace that grips a smouldering turf bed,
We step into the reality of fiction.

And that wrecked ship's timber, the fraction
Of the whole, lintel to brace a livelihood,
Stone house left to the coast's contraction.

What lime mortar holds an old world in train?
What shape locked out such ocean-seasoned wood?
We step into the reality of fiction.

A lick of paint faded on the lintel, fading stain
Of landfall or landlocked embrace of blood-red,
Stone house left to the coast's contraction.

Edge of country that will or won't take you in,
Lost worlds burn chilled, abandoned.
We step into the reality of fiction,
Stone house left to the coast's contraction.

## DAY AFTER THE STORM

*'sky still boiling'*
JOHN D'ALTON

Clouds draw energy and give back rain
Over Goat Island in Long Island Bay,
And the clouds reset the sky's *tain*.

All gods want payback, all gods retain
Their grip – the centre of their claim is grey.
Clouds draw energy and give back rain.

Teachers helped children home as the wind vane
Buckled on its high place – dark smudge on the radar –
And the clouds reset the sky's *tain*.

But in the aftermath the broken world realigns
Reports from outside, from others' Doomsdays,
Clouds draw energy and give back rain.

Outside Newman's Café, we hear a refrain:
'The sky's still boiling'; though tones downplay
And the clouds reset the sky's *tain*.

While the ruffled current drags the channel's stone,
A hundreds gannets test the hundred isles of Carbery,
Clouds draw energy and give back rain
And the clouds reset the sky's *tain*.

## BETWEEN PIER AND ISLANDS

The steady-unsteady pushing away from pier
As ferry departs for islands and herring gulls float
Over rolled waters that will rough in time for it to reappear.

Cloud builds to join islands to canopy where few trees clear
chimneys of broken farmhouses and dead castle parapets.
The steady-unsteady pushing away from pier.

Between pier and islands a shoal of fish passes clear
to blur in weed and blotting of sun – halfway between slates.
Over rolled waters that will rough in time for it to reappear.

Reset after storms the mirror fur of the seal and otter,
the toxins of a clean and repainted hull, a fishnet float.
The steady-unsteady pushing away from pier.

Even left behind because once gone its pier to pier,
the slightest ripple is an address to the film that transmits;
Over rolled waters that will rough in time for it to reappear.

But ferries leave long gaps between knots of winter-
Crossings, and a stranded passenger is lost to lobster pots –
The steady-unsteady pushing away from pier
Over rolled waters that will rough in time for it to reappear.

## RED SHED RED BARN DICHOTOMY [FROM WHEATBELT WESTERN AUSTRALIA TO KNOX COUNTY, OHIO]

This is one saying that won't relocate –
'on opposites sides of the world
red shed is as to red barn' is simply inaccurate.

Red shed is bulky but low-peaked without a hayloft,
red barn back there was aspirational if not spiritualised –
and this is one saying that won't relocate.

There's the issue of building materials and patents,
of ad-hoc, makeshift, prefabricated, and what's to hand,
red shed is as to red barn is simply inaccurate.

There's the issue of uniformity, the site specific, the template
of local traditions, the presence or lack of tourists, farm *vs* the land;
this is one saying that won't relocate.

But the red shed of metal in a storm that would translate
across the frisson of hemispheres, calls for wooden walls and lightning rods!
Red shed is as to red barn is simply inaccurate.

What values they hold are the same and different,
what they contain or shelter is mutually desired;
this is one saying that won't relocate –
*red shed is as to red barn* is simply inaccurate.

## THE LITTLE BLACK CORMORANT TREE

*for Tracy*

Dozens of little black cormorants daylight roosting
on the dead-in-the-lake tree with its duckweed halo
the suburbs close around them with stilled ibises watching.

These cormorants are florets open and closed, some contemplating
difference as close friends dry their wings, the ß-keratins offering sap-flow –
dozens of little black cormorants daylight roosting.

Between the lakeshore and an islet, the cormorant tree is preparing
for mass ascension, that lift of surprise or agitation, a threat that rows
through suburbs close around it with stilled ibises watching.

So many encounters with humans who can't reach its branching
into the close air of all-breath, held together by slick diving birds of shared ego –
dozens of little black cormorants daylight roosting.

Its weight of numbers shows the faith of death's shaping –
the ringwork of growth that adds invisibly after the scherzo,
the suburbs close around them with stilled ibises watching.

White ibises fall to haunches to study behaviour of the tree in its weirding
way of life in death its offering of sanctuary, monopoly, expo!
Dozens of little black cormorants daylight roosting
as suburbs close around them with stilled ibises watching.

## WATERING THE TREES

*i.m. W. S. Merwin*


It's hot late afternoon and I am watering trees
using the zigzag technique to handle the gradient –
this is no survivalist act but one of constancy.

Magpies are gathering where a humidity
rises from the ring of watering before being lost to the heat –
it's hot late afternoon and I am watering trees.

Swamp Yates planted a few years ago cease
to change sun into life, retreating to the craving of roots –
this is no survivalist act but one of constancy.

We've enough water in our 'tree tank' to do maybe
six more of these waterings, then we lose all to the drought –
it's hot late afternoon and I am watering trees.

But I will never stop trying to lift the trees
to eye level and higher, to climb against the new climate –
this is no survivalist act but one of constancy.

Nothing in me is elevated in making sanctuary
and the body stress is neither penance nor punishment –
it's hot late afternoon and I am watering trees
this is no survivalist act but one of constancy.

Leconte de Lisle
**VILLANELLE**

*A dark night, during a calm, beneath the Equator*


Time, Number, Expanse
Have fallen from the dark sky
Into the sombre sea's stillness.

Shroud of shadow and silence,
The darkness erases absolutely
Time, Number, Expanse.

Like heavy, dumb debris,
Mind plunges into the void's dormancy,
Into the sombre sea's stillness.

In itself, with itself, all is darkness,
Dream, feeling, memory,
Time, Number, Expanse,
Into the sombre sea's stillness.

*translated by John Kinsella*

## EXAMINE THYSELF, SINGING HONEYEATER

Examine thyself, singing honeyeater
attended and not harried by half-a-dozen
silvereyes flurrying excitedly about this loner.

Alone this singing honeyeater comes in over
the hills and paddocks, into geraniums, is all meditation –
examine thyself, singing honeyeater!

Alone this singing honeyeater is a singer
of a differing song with greater and lesser syllables drawn on –
silvereyes flurrying excitedly about this loner.

It was surely part of a flock or a pair,
it surely hasn't spent life since the nest alone from its 'own' –
examine thyself, singing honeyeater?

But what if it has – that is, been self-contained, a recluse, an outsider?
What if it prefers the company of silvereyes or other associations?
Silvereyes flurrying excitedly about this loner.

Large among the small birds weighing down the flower
and twig, feathers ruffled as singing an infinite canon –
examine thyself, singing honeyeater, and rejoice in silver-
eyes flurrying excitedly about your character.

## MOTH LIES DOWN

Moth lies down to die and fossilise
hardening body parts with emphasis,
last breath to set its shape on soft surface.

When the semi-arid is converted to marshiness,
the downrush a switch of grit to oasis,
so moth lies down to die and fossilise.

The fossil record is light on moths and butterflies,
but moth at end of life looks to what lies
via last breath to set its shape on soft surface.

The letting-go of softness to privilege carapace,
a sigh for eggs laid its cocoon opening, the release,
moth lies down to die and fossilise.

A decision made in an instant wings relax
and a hundred million years seems a chance,
via last breath to set its shape on soft surface.

But old ways brought down through the interface
don't expect the tomb to explain the ethics –
moth lies down to die and fossilise
last breath to set its shape on soft surface.

## THE EASTER LILIES

It's so dry they lack colour though flush in the blank air –
'redneck' colonial upset, the bliss of hope outweighing the irony,
who knows what they reach for if light isn't sustenance and repair.

There's no correlation between our body and its stem, bare
skin and petals, and to suggest otherwise seems a selfish plenty,
it's so dry they lack colour though flush in the blank air.

In quelled light heart-in-the-mouth not on-the-sleeve puts lie
    to a *language of flowers*,
to illustrations pressing on blooms laid too thick against beds – threnodies –
who knows what they reach for if light isn't sustenance and repair.

But really they bulb over root half in and half out of a rhythm they stir
against the empty rain-gauge, but we wait, wait as hope not ceremony,
it's so dry they lack colour though flush in the blank air.

At their boldest when early rains have opened clay's pores,
they demand a description but even then there's no offering, no artistry –
who knows what they reach for if light isn't sustenance and repair.

*Overcast* is the false promise and a wanting and denying of solar
urges – they glance away and cannot face each other, this fallacy!
It's so dry they lack colour though flush in the blank air –
who knows what they reach for if light isn't sustenance and repair.

## SUNSKINK VILLANELLESQUE

A sunskink dropped bronze at your feet
    not in worship but dismay –
a misstep in its pursuit of the sun its thirst for heat.

As copper to bronze its lightning burst,
    its dazzling pursuit of barely-aware-prey –
a misstep in its pursuit of the sun its thirst for heat.

That dash while recharging, that meet and greet
    with quickening teeth, upside down writhe-twist geometry,
such that a sunskink dropped bronze upright at your feet.

But alarm is the pulse in the throat and threat
    is deduced from dismay whatever you think of integrity
as misstep in its pursuit of the sun its thirst for heat.

Firm on four feet as the predator that would consume *it*,
    but not as one predator is to another as affinity –
no, *just* a sunskink dropped bronze at your feet.

Just there under the shadecloth taking in what
    sun can force through, and sudden as gnomon or deity,
    a sunskink dropped bronze at your feet,
a misstep in its pursuit of the sun its thirst for heat.

## MORTALITY

This is what's to hand wherever we turn,
unseen colours of a spectrum we mark time by,
shadow catching up with us outside the sun.

Days lengthening and shortening, unravelling seasons,
a thornbill feeding beyond the window that is not the same thornbill
    as yesterday;
this is what's to hand wherever we turn.

All that red dust stirred up and redistributed, strewn,
all that red dust coating our lungs, an idea of history –
shadow catching up with us outside the sun.

The circumference of a great rainwater tank is a chron-
ometer of 'settlement', its silver cover the facade of our body water
    whereby
we claim what's to hand wherever we turn.

Can I speak for us in saying a magpie scanned by the dawn
might say nothing we would desire but can be interpreted as lullaby?
Shadow catching up with it outside the sun?

A decade marked on topography and we still look to learn
what our impact might or might not be, well past our heyday?
This is what's to hand wherever we turn,
shadow catching up with us outside the sun.

## THE EXPANDING PHRASE: WHEN *THEY* MANIPULATE THE DATA

Clouds that weigh down a clear sky might be hard to see,
but nascent is the future that suits and binds the audience,
the thornbills' usual pace is still rapid as heresy.

What is claimed will be believed from jealousy
in the latter stages of the smorgasbord since
clouds that weigh down a clear sky might be hard to see.

It loads up that moisture that visual innumeracy,
to preserve ourselves from a dry dam-burst's distress,
the thornbills' usual pace is still rapid as heresy.

For example, a few days ago near Picnic Hill territory,
a dust devil aimed for a house and tore out its presence,
clouds that weigh down a clear sky might be hard to see.

For example, people keep records that thrive on inaccuracy
to use as evidence of a different set of climactic conditions –
the thornbills' usual pace is still rapid as heresy.

All these lines of termites and gravel ants and the tendency
of plaster board to crack as the house expands and contracts is evidence
that clouds weighing down a clear sky are hard to see,
that thornbills' usual pace is still rapid as heresy.

## 'EXPIRY' DATES


These heirloom seeds past their 'expiry' date
or 'best use by' or 'before' to soften the blow,
brought out of the dry dark and planted late.

Late in the day late in a season we calibrate
by the idea of seasons, pushed below,
these heirloom seeds past their 'expiry' date.

A history of healthiest seeds from plants
let go to seed conjures the strains of a sun halo,
brought out of the dry dark and planted late.

As if the journey timed to the year has spent
its accruals and longevity, with only emptiness to follow,
these heirloom seeds past their 'expiry' date.

Organic harmonies of leaf, stem and root,
or a blank garden bed or shape of seed in soil a hollow –
brought out of the dry dark and planted late.

These seeds that insects might annihilate,
these seeds that might never have passed through,
these heirloom seeds past their 'expiry' date
brought out of the dry dark and planted late.

## PRECISE LANGUAGE

It's not a thesaurus issue but one of quiddity,
*the dangling blob* of web the stretch of silken thread
that has long forgotten its creator's spinneret.

It dangles dirty with dust and the dead from the transom secularity
near-centre of the suppressed gothic gable roof of the red shed,
it's not a thesaurus issue but one of quiddity.

Though it's an imprecise and disturbing entity,
there's specificity in each spent insect's exoskeleton entangled,
having long forgotten its destroyer's spinneret.

You walk into *it* and it consumes your face as its ancient polity
is declared – an eschatology a brush with the entombed – suspended –
it's not a thesaurus issue but one of quiddity.

You know it's the massive web of an orb weaver that made a deity
of its sequence of insects dead on a thread and left as its final word –
having long forgotten the lexicon of its own spinneret.

Which word do you search for in overcoming abjection's levity,
a ghost train moment of willing suspension, an oddness so overstated?
It's not a thesaurus issue but one of quiddity
that has been forgotten beyond its creator's spinneret.

## DEMI-SURREALIST VILLANELLE

*for Peter*


It doesn't bend to the shimmer of feather
it talks against strands plucked for the nest,
a stunned silence isn't aphasia which is no less a measure.

*Bronze!* on a downturned limb is never
lacklustre or overstated, but caught by sun it hesitates,
and doesn't bend to the coruscation of feather.

It's not retreat into loops of corner of a corner –
a pleasure-seeking in-theatre escaping its forest,
a stunned silence isn't aphasia which is no less a measure.

For describing something true to life – a splinter
to insert under breathless skin – the allergy owns a scratchtest;
it doesn't bend to the fulguration of feather.

Not to be stunned into silence, not to take a breather,
the implications of naming and denoting a star ornithologist,
a stunned silence isn't aphasia which is no less a measure.

But when flight is taken from a tenuous perch of uphill boulders,
and horn is woven as hair and hair to claw daub a personal best,
it doesn't bend to the shimmer of feather's
stunned silence which is no less a measure.

## LIMBO

*'E vegno in parte ove non è che luca.'*
DANTE, INFERNO CANTO 4


In the valley we ride down the mist to where it's glitterless
despite the brook despite the spectral feathers of that kingfisher,
for each pre-invasion tree is cut down to a lightless emptiness.

These themes of recurrence that conjoin Dante and Virgil and Liszt
and Coleridge and Dante in a patriarchal tryst a lopsided atmosphere
in the valley we ride down the mist to where it's glitterless.

As viewing takes more than a viewer can give as they scrutinise,
as they subtract from what's been condemned as going nowhere,
for each ancient tree is cut down to a flightless emptiness.

But *nowhere* is not here and *here* is where essence
defies Kantian categories, the moon filthy with probes and rovers,
in the valley we ride down the mist to where it's glitterless.

What we take from where it seems available as address
and praise – a limp gratitude inside us to surrogate for repair,
for each pre-'settlement' tree is cut down to such lightless emptiness?

But no more than waking to see a rearrangement of cosmos
to note fresh constructions of roads and antonyms of nature –
in the valley we ride down the mist to where it's glitterless,
for each ancient tree is cut down to flightless emptiness.

## INVERTED PASTORAL VILLANELLE OF FREESIAS

The twists of ancestry in the effaced –
a making way for *fresh* denotations of *constructing*.
Freesias edge paths of occlusion
and defy pasture's naturalisation.

    I disassociate my grandmother's fascination
    for a garland of freshness and fugitive gathering,
    halfway engaging pasture's naturalisation:

for they won't burst sweet with inversion,
grow as angels in a reverse enrapturing,
for freesias edge paths of occlusion.

    They don't flower fragrant in harmonic tension
    with exhaust fumes and timber milling,
    nor defy pasture's naturalisation.

A politics of *ICBMs* is deracination
in laying raw the unearthing,
freesias edge paths of occlusion.

    Freesias edge paths of occlusion
    at the very limit of muckraking
    to disrupt pasture's naturalisation.

## GESTE MISCUE: PREDICTING THE HARVEST

Don't look to the title for a lead, a making of sense –
the miscue is vocabulary without syntax, sans dryness
where there is no water in the table nor on the surface.

The geste of an epic's failure is the dead unstuck in its enterprise –
a momentous suck on the dried well, the lewd plural of bureaucracies.
Don't look to the title for a lead, a making of sense.

If journey is a motif of ripples, then red dirt reformed along clearances
un-tithes property along those lewd and ludicrous tables of virtues
where there is no water in the table nor on the surface.

Governance of chivalries – such intoxicating leaps of credence –
takes us to the department of ears (*now* in anthesis) and bushels and hectares;
but don't look to the title for a lead, a making of census.

Hightail out of the slump, ride the crest but beware of oncoming trucks,
for the traversals of tales and their gestures is an atoning for distance,
especially where there is no water in the table nor on the surface.

A thirst still being most of what will makes up those bodies
to flounder in the volatile smut of cylindrical storage centres,
please don't look to the title for a lead, a making of sense –
where there is no water in the table nor on the surface.

## ADDICTIONS

When something calls to you and you think you're calling it,
and the craving is a slip between craven and caving in,
the definition of animate and inanimate shift.

To fall to an addiction is to *get* at all costs,
to score is to brag that you've conquered the mountain,
when something calls to you and you think you're calling it.

To call an addiction positive is a case of *needs must*,
to pursue the cliché as the lexical exception
such that the definition of animate and inanimate shift.

The consequences are what's stacked up in God we Trust,
with gradations from porn to chocolate to prayer or heroin –
when something calls to you and you think you're calling it.

To feed a need is to measure your content,
caught in the paradox of need for privacy and attention,
such that the definition of animate and inanimate shift.

These addictive behaviours that come before and after augment
the resist or fall *fait accompli* all or nothing infatuation –
when something calls to you and you think you're calling it,
the definition of animate and inanimate shift.

## SHUFFLEWING FAMILY

If the valley can contain togetherness and disruption,
the juvenile emphasises what a parent is doing –
leaf dashed against branch to tear open a cocoon.

There's no room for observing but there is for description
as if one is subjective and the other scientific, a subterfuge –
as if the valley can contain togetherness and disruption.

See their forms swoop between old eucalypts and between
fragments of song that anneal into a singing –
leaf dashed against branch to tear open a cocoon.

From inside, the flight reshapes imprint to sunshine,
we can't hand over their operating specs, their feeding,
as if the valley can contain wandering and disruption.

Sticking together as a trio, the valley a fraction
of presence, a fraction of potential, a fraction of meaning –
leaf dashed against branch to tear open a cocoon.

But nothing is constrained by the awkwardness between generations,
and branch-settling is also leafy wave of the name *shufflewing*;
if the valley can contain togetherness and disruption,
leaf dashed against branch tears open a cocoon.

## COLLECTING TIM FROM HIS SCHOOL BUS STOP 60 KS AWAY

What is distance in cost to the circulatory system of Earth,
but to keep our one vehicle travel to a bare minimum
in our relative isolation trying to stay close to our fireless hearth?

Down the loop I saw a young mulga snake and thought it death –
not death from its strike – king browns' one of the deadliest venoms –
what is distance in cost to the circulatory system of Earth? –

but thought death because it was inert and maybe struck by the truth
of driving, the brutality of wheels; though it seems not to have left the
    forum,
of our relative isolation trying to stay close to our fireless hearth.

With grasses eaten away in the long dry, mice have opened a vacuum,
and mice-numbers falling away mulga snake hunts further afield beset
    by jim-jams,
so what is distance in cost to the circulatory system of Earth?

I saw many alpacas mob a slow-moving utility bearing a haybale
    shibboleth,
and I saw galahs harvesting dust along scoured furrows of the odium,
extramural to our relative isolation trying to stay close to our fireless
    hearth.

If it's a periphery we occupy it still feels like the centre of a system
that requires all or nothing of us, that tangles and untangles isopleths –
but what is distance in cost to the circulatory system of Earth,
in our relative isolation trying to stay close to our fireless hearth?

**CORELLAS, HILL, TOWN, AND THE FACT THAT BEYOND MOUNT OMMENEY, OUT OF SIGHT AND HEARING OF THE VIEWER/LISTENER, IS THE YONGAH HILL DETENTION CENTRE**


I sit and wait on the corner looking up the aerials of Mount Ommaney
and hear a flock of corellas conversing intensely down in the funnel
of valley where salt sclera hold pools of river in myotic empathy.

The further the flock moves away the louder it gets in sympathy
with those who cannot see but guess its pattern and path, its passional.
I sit and wait on the corner looking up the aerials of Mount Ommaney.

I belong to the faith of feather and flight as searcher for euphony,
but I know the flock might be shot when it lifts to bare stubble hills
of valley where salt sclera hold pools of river in myotic empathy.

This town that centres our compass – food and medical and a litany
of services that 'regional' compels us towards, the gravitational pull.
I sit and wait on the corner looking up the aerials of Mount Ommaney.

Between me and the tips of the steel masts a single corella making rapidly
for the invisible but noisy flock – erratic flight, but driven and radical –
down to valley where salt sclera hold pools of river in myotic empathy.

Such landscapes open in moments of waiting when you synch a telepathy
between the edge of town and what would remain outside its demesne, its catchall;
I sit and wait on the corner looking up the aerials of Mount Ommaney
while down in the valley salt sclera hold pools of river in myotic empathy.

## THE TERMITES

The termites move slow but fast in their own fashion –
when *all is said and done* they get where they are going,
when the house shakes gently on mutable foundations.

Interior signs are poorly marked but we gasp at exterior signs –
mud galleries to a woody future, soldiers of the colony rattling on song,
the termites move slow but fast in their own fashion.

Everything shifts within the dynamic of a house broken-
down – digested and turned to frass – the termites progressing,
when the house shakes gently on mutable foundations.

How far have they reached, how far have they gone?
Listen to them define their own building codes, their rites from wrongs,
the termites move slow but fast in their own fashion.

Everything changes fast against the slow intrusion,
the breaking and entering, the spiritualist vanishings,
when the house shakes gently on mutable foundations.

So much history – personal and otherwise – so much speculation
and investment in dwelling hollowed to a lick of paint, to underwriting,
the termites move slow but fast in their own fashion –
when the house shakes gently on mutable foundations.

## FRESH ECHIDNA DIGGINGS

It's not an exhumation it's a revelation
of the subterranean to the force of light
if they survive the tongue the extraction.

Light unwanted a breaching of the under- *wynd* or *twitten*
'settler' equivalence, the carry of pulp beneath granites,
it's not an exhumation it's a revelation.

We get a thrill to see evidence of the determination
of echidna returned to the arena, tracking termites
which will rarely survive the tongue the extraction.

What is the paradox the conundrum the repetition
of crisis and peace and quandary making tautologies despite
and because of it not being an exhumation but a revelation?

Quilled low-to-ground shaker-up of tubes and kitchens,
boudoirs and galleries: we invest degrees of health when echidna is on site,
though termites will rarely survive the tongue the extraction.

A hideous saying we could hide below – *someone's
loss being another's gain* – fresh bloody ground, open-cut:
it's not an exhumation it's a revelation,
if they survive the tongue the extraction.

## LATE REPTILE APPEARANCES

Late reptile appearances are always early now
as long sleeps are something they won't know,
head to tail the seasons link as today's tomorrow.

It's fundamental that a denier will mention the crow,
drag it into 'same old same old' picture as a species that can *come* and *go*,
but late reptile appearances are always early now.

As long as the slaughterhouses are fed sheep / pig / cow,
the twists of art and acquisitiveness will follow,
head to tail the seasons link as today's tomorrow.

Each parcel of land each string of words allow
the bank to mortgage posterity – capital's timeless argot –
late reptile appearances are always early now.

Of scales and eggs and live young and cold blood and claws
gripping the bricks and mortar and a winter-sun's glow,
head to tail the seasons link as today's tomorrow.

And there's a local who says, 'The snake can't sleep now
so it can't wake when it should, it grows tired with what follows' –
late reptile appearances are always early now
head to tail the seasons link as today's tomorrow.

## OUTSIDE COLONIAL SEASONING: AN INCULCATED 'FOLK TALE'

'spring came during winter here – we had 30 degree centigrade days in august, and, indeed today is over 30. bizarre and disturbing. all is yellow with apocalyptic blossom. the snakes are out – confused, hungry, moving out of their usual physical patternings.'

*from a note to Susan Stewart*


Spring came mid-winter
and days were hot as snake days
yellow with apocalyptic flowers

Deter the blue tongue skink deter
it from the warm road and an earlier death-day,
spring came mid-winter

Who speaks the category speaks thermometer
as pollen rains hot and fast and shifts grey,
yellow with apocalyptic flowers

Silver-eyes are seen changing the structure
of nests outside evolutionary sway
spring came mid-winter

It's not polite to offer a cure a spider
eating its shadow a logorrhoea a tongue-tie or stay
yellow with apocalyptic flowers

Reaction catalyst / scatter gather
index gametes mucous membrane affray –
spring came mid-winter
yellow with apocalyptic flowers.

## GIANT INFLATABLE SLIDE ATOP A HILL IN THE WHEATBELT

The giant inflatable slide on the hill
deceives first like a mining shaft's headframe –
set in a high clearing amongst stubble.

If wind lifts it will tilt at a windmill
whose blade spins to draw deep water and tame
the giant inflatable slide on the hill.

Can breath of seven hundred sheep fill
the slide with fun as per a farmer's aim,
set in a high clearing amongst stubble?

From a perch across the valley distil
an essence of play – dirt bikes and the claim
of a giant inflatable slide on the hill.

A hullaballoo – guests rise & fall,
dive, tumble and entangle – same old same
high in a high clearing amongst stubble.

As tethers strain, and ghost of crop needles,
slide threatens to fly or undermine fame –
that deflating once giant slide on the hill
set in a high clearing amongst stubble.

## AN ANNUAL MEETING AT THE YORK AGRICULTURAL SHOW

Zebra finches galvanic localised fire without burning trees
in full-blown speed-dating song just as we interpreted last year,
so many birds making a go of nesting against the tensity.

Zebra finches work the odds, adjust as they can to sprees
of pesticide and herbicide, the contraction of their sphere,
zebra finches galvanic localised fire without burning trees.

Rides and displays are rising and falling in spring glory,
as if everything is as it should be, as if it fits the agricultural calendar,
so many birds making a go of nesting against the tensity.

Declarations are coming thick and fast, the okays
to keep on pouring glyphosate as Best Wheat Sheaf of Show flickers,
zebra finches galvanic localised fire without burning trees.

The intensity of many small birds conversing and hopping lee-
ward to the face of an ever so gentle breeze through tents of conservative
    *pollies*,
so many birds making a go of nesting against the tensity.

This is community say the zebra finches which you're free
to hear if you want to hear even though you so often ignore
so many birds making a go of nesting against the tensity,
as zebra finches galvanise fire without burning trees.

## RECUSED VILLANELLE

Who are we to judge affiliations of seed and beak
in the dispersal of drying out – *be grateful there was rain* –
calling me out to leave the shelter of a windbreak?

I am rust of harried earth as I climb the firebreak,
and though I fluster at the coating I cannot delete the stain –
who are we to judge affiliations of seed and beak?

The question of waking to a world that declares work
a panacea that will keep revolutions in synch with their refrain –
calling me out to leave the shelter of a windbreak.

Will you or I ever break free of agri-pastoral rip-off rhetoric
without an interrogation of the rules of speech, the lapse of pronouns –
who are we to judge affiliations of seed and beak?

The emphasis is on a thornbill picking up after mowing's fake
declarations of synthesis – seed not complete falling and plucked fine –
calling me out to leave the shelter of a windbreak.

Absolve and observe, in the scene and wandering away, for the sake
of waking to a day of 'purpose' that transubstantiates pain –
who am I to judge affiliations of seed and beak
calling us out to leave the shelter of a windbreak?

## INNER-WORKINGS

It came from within a tree long dead
cut down to a wedge of trunk and phantom limbs,
termite-tunnelled centre forking and offering no lead.

It came from a cut alongside the nail of an index finger pointed
at nowhere in particular, but pointed as I exclaim
that it came from within a tree long dead.

It came from the spring sprung from an old
clock, a wind-up always imperfect keeper of time –
termite-tunnelled centre forking and offering no lead.

It came from an interest in precisely *what* was said
and what was *meant* by the empowered in the offence of their claim,
as it came from within a tree long dead.

It came from the mushroom burnt by light – unturned
so its gills sought earth in sky and withered calling for seraphim,
termite-tunnelled centre forking and offering no lead.

It came from refrain, that desperate searching for the planned,
the patterned, the plotted, the finely-drawn diagram:
it came from within a tree long dead
termite-tunnelled centre forking and offering no lead.

## UNDER SEDATION – 'COMING TO' WITH REARRANGEMENTS

What we emerge to out of twilit sleep:
an adjustment we make as blue wrens twitch
when time without memory is called a 'slip'.

To deform words for the bracket creep
of life-loss as experience accumulates into a 'fix',
when time without memory is called a 'slip'.

It's the blue wren's separate life we strip
of its autonomy as we impose prefix and suffix*,
the *what* we emerge to out of twilit sleep.

What was said when 'under' might be a hope
that your specialist-confessor will never relinquish,
when time without memory is called a 'slip'.

To fight the call of the drug is the wren over the crop,
is the shadow to the tree, is the hay dancing antics,
what we emerge to out of twilit sleep.

But so many pass through the wards of gossip,
so many voices speak small birds as a wing and a stitch;
when time without memory is called a 'slip'
we phase into the picture out of twilit sleep.


*semiautonomous / autonomously...?

# TESTAMENT

I cannot remember before I was born and might not after I pass,
the endangered species that made a comeback before I lapse
will grow with me in my silence when the planet is my flesh.

For I will be more present after than before, and each fresh
breath of animal or plant will be one that complements remorse –
I cannot remember before I was born and might not after I pass.

The planet becomes the body I once had, and the senses I once
called my own but shared, and the living hurt is the shade's relapse
which will grow with me in my silence when the planet is my flesh.

And in the same way I had a predictable vocabulary and syntax,
my post-life will flow like food through the body, walk familiar track –
I cannot remember before I was born and might not after I pass.

Afterlife is wearing the planet as flesh, a stony and creeping flesh
as the only flesh you can have when you set adrift from your forms,
will grow with me in my silence when the planet is my flesh.

The clouds bundled on the fall-away of valley, the rash
of storm sunset to reset climate, and always those birds of difference –
I cannot remember before I was born and might not after I pass
what will grow with me in my silence when the planet is my flesh.

## GECKOES IN DAYLIGHT HOURS

Wheatbelt stone gecko keeps its tail
as the box it shelters in is disturbed within the red shed,
but the marbled gecko drops its tail

when a half-brick is lifted to reveal
or expose its sanctuary and what's on its mind,
whereas wheatbelt stone gecko kept its tail.

Euphony of body is a glut of insects in the dead
of night by a light it alone comprehends,
but the marbled gecko drops its tail

as it is surprised and alarmed in its 'room reveal',
a peal of fleshy interests ringing soundlessly,
whereas wheatbelt stone gecko kept its tail.

And I, the unwitting instigator, who am fascinated
by the colour and texture and heartbeat visibility –
am troubled by the defence of a marbled gecko dropping its tail.

All that storage lost while exposed to the sun,
reptiles of night under brick and in shed – complementary but solitary –
but while wheatbelt stone gecko keeps its tail
        the marbled gecko drops its tail.

## ANXIETY VILLANELLE: OUT OF KILTER

Cicada on flywire over angled window of valley
prepositions to locate our flows and tendencies of view –
though in its stillness it might fly before singing ferociously.

The moon in its waning was covered in leaves and lichen,
but the moon in its waning is losing its vegetable hew –
cicada on flywire over angled window of valley

Degrees of anxiety are dust on the inside – or anteriorly-
speaking you are coughing up ruptured ground, tried untrue –
though in its stillness it might flee before singing ferociously.

The sun is cut off from looking directly to *the scene*, but fully
engages with the 'light of day' as a set of circadian clues –
cicada on flywire over angled window of valley.

Propositions to extend an argument from an exoskeletal folly
of forms, the indoors / outdoors binary, our cataclysm of the new –
though in its stillness it might fly before singing ferociously.

A formula of observation to surprise and yet fit an anomaly
of agitation and meditation with the frame of *you* blocking-in a purview –
cicada on flywire over angled window of valley,
though in its stillness it might fly before singing ferociously.

## JAM TREE GULLY

*for Tracy*


Insects erupt out of thick, lime-green grass –
a flying up that is escape *and* expedition;
a flying up that is full-on engagement.

A *guess where* the brown honeyeaters nest? – but don't verify;
expect the sun skink to glow on the sleeper, hold back the dirt.
Insects erupt out of thick, lime-green grass.

As branches beyond windows extend,
angles stay roughly the same, though arms lengthen;
a flying up that is full-on engagement.

And the shy sun orchid is reconstituting,
though proof of its flowering is slightly withheld –
insects erupt out of thick, lime-green grass.

It's not that we want it to be one and the same,
but for the same to have scope to change –
a flying up that is full-on engagement.

Air is the most stable imprint, and air always laments –
a scorpion fly, a painted lady, at the interchange –
insects erupt out of thick, lime-green grass,
a flying up that is full-on engagement.

## HAILSTONE VILLANELLE

Hailstones in misshapen formation pound on roof corrugations,
distorted in scrying before reaching their target,
feathers and leaves stripped, birds and trees in transition.

To taste the fracture when air pressure is shaken and unshaken,
and lightning brings its personalised thunder close to a house in retreat,
hailstones misshapen in formation pound on the roof's corrugations.

What can you portend when there are no signs of exposition,
when as sudden as sky the ground is remade as ice in white heat?
Feathers and leaves stripped, birds and trees in remission.

Which feather belongs to which absent bird, how did it pattern
a flight path laid bare to updraft the wet into frozen conflict?
Hailstones in misshapen formation pound on the roof's corrugations.

Jagged as quartz exposed in red earth after the deluge's erosion,
violent as an orbuculum's sheen of hope broken by its clairvoyant,
feathers and leaves stripped as birds and trees are lost in transition.

Milky-centred fist-sized stones resist melting after devastation –
each leaf green as when torn away, strips of bark clean as skin, feathers rent;
hailstones in misshapen formation pound on the roof's corrugations,
feathers and leaves, stripped birds and trees in remission.

## DAMAGE SLOWLY REVEALS ITSELF

Damage slowly reveals itself days after the storm,
and there's a *whiff of animal death* on the wind,
the full extent of the change made evident in the post-mortem.

Just to have survived the hyperbole, the exordium
of a rewriting of all we'd hoped to rescind,
damage slowly reveals itself days after the storm.

The lines of traversal across the hill torn from their forms,
fresh gullies opened and old gullies collapsed,
the full extent of the change made evident in the post-mortem.

We are not the only people affected – insurance claims
are filed across a band of the valley – recounted and signed –
damage slowly reveals itself days after the storm.

Down in town the supermarket blossoms a spectrum
of impacts – wrecked roof, smashed patio, *messing with my mind,*
the full extent of the change made evident in the post-mortem.

Because it's like that, picking up the pieces after a game
played outside the rules, language an effort to reframe, reimagine.
Damage slowly reveals itself days after the storm,
the full extent of the change made evident in the post-mortem.

## DISORDERED VILLANELLE OF THE OWLET NIGHTJAR OUTSIDE THE WINDOW

The call is not to let us know but to speak around us,
the owlet nightjar perched on the dead hyoid trunk just beyond
vertical blinds where moths eat light seeping out from the limits.

I can't see it but its shape appears in memory and we process
it processing territory and family and hunger scanning the domain,
vertical blinds where moths eat light seeping out from the limits.

It doesn't need us to know it's there but we need to feel it's of us,
the feathers that line the inside of our skin, the diet that's so alien,
the call is not to let us know but to speak around us.

We don't search for reflection that's not there because we don't stress
where there should be unstressed syllables, this blending with the lined
vertical blinds where moths eat light seeping out from the limits.

I don't know what darkness is if I can sense it, and light is a trace
of rufous flight from the earth or dusty hollow caught in a half yawn
as the call is not to let us know but to speak around us.

The ripple of excitement inside these rooms as it operates darkness,
casting aside atlas moths that can't shelter inside glass or behind screens –
vertical blinds where moths eat light seeping out from the limits
and the call is not to let us know but to speak around us.

## AGAINST WHITE SUPREMACISTS CO-OPTING DYLAN THOMAS'S 'DO NOT GO GENTLE INTO THAT GOOD NIGHT'


Lines taken out of context can make darkness burn
For those who want to burn the world, but darkness
Is their slow burn, white lies their eruption.

And when leaflets fostering discrimination
Appear outside a wheatbelt supermarket, they gloss
Lines taken out of context and make a darkness burn.

But what most disturbs is that such leaflets remain
Or are browsed as the town broods under a glaze of tolerance –
Is it a slow burn before white lies trigger an eruption?

We share breath and relish the health to rise each day in turn,
Each day shared in sameness and difference,
But lines taken out of context can make darkness burn.

Every word of intolerance sold as 'warning' is the crimson
Shade of the day-to-day accretion of a rage that is not the rage for existence –
A slow burn, white lies their corruption.

Let words of life that urge a life continue to be a lexicon
Of day and night, light and dark, of overlaps in time's ingress –
Lines taken out of context can make darkness burn,
A slow burn, white lies their corruption.

## A VILLANELLE'S SILENCE: A RECLAIMING

*for those murdered in the Christchurch mosques*


For those who knew each name as it spoke a person,
for those who know each person by names they now hear,
we come together in a silence of prayer that stretches horizons.

What we share is the resistance to violence, the negation
of hatred and prejudice, each word to be felt and not lost in the familiar,
for those who knew each name as it spoke a person.

As light finds its way through the veins of the leaf, season
meets season in the growth of the sacred, an open space where
we come together in a silence of prayer that stretches horizons.

To walk together or walk past with or without recognition,
but to walk past with sacred respect, the shape of the living figure,
for those who knew each name as it spoke a person.

Never forget and always let light fall on the smallest portion
of neglect, those little incidents we forget, the smallest slights that adhere –
rather, we come together in a silence of prayer that stretches horizons.

But those who kill cannot undo the life of the spirit – they might imagine
there are those who will hate along with them, but they are wrong,
    cannot plant fear;
and we come together in a silence of prayer that stretches horizons
for those who knew each name as it spoke a person.

## ABSENCE

'I turned to share the transport'
        WILLIAM WORDSWORTH, 'Surprised by Joy'


A rock tumbled down and shed its lichen skin,
it came loose with heavy rain after ligaments had atrophied,
and now it rests behind the house having lost momentum.

I expected a message nothing to do with environs,
nothing to do with symbiotic organisms or small birds,
as a rock tumbled down and shed its lichen skin.

And I had you close by to share the surprise and need for action –
a new condition of risk, a warning, a need to hold rocks back from
    a landslide.
And now it rests behind the house having lost momentum.

These segues of now and then, these stories around the kitchen –
those who we loved and those we lost and always respected –
so a rock tumbled down and shed its lichen skin.

It could have rolled further it could have risen
to the occasion with potential, the impact of an asteroid,
but it came to rest behind the house having lost momentum.

But that's what I mean when I say I turn
expecting a message from our dead friend –
a rock tumbled down and shed its lichen skin,
and now it rests behind the house having lost momentum.

## I HEAR ACROSS THE VALLEYS AND GNARLED HILLS

I hear across the valleys and gnarled hills
a strong echo I don't know and won't know,
of having a grandchild approaching its landfall.

There are few terms of reference outside dam walls
and metaphors of water that lap at broken vows
across ancient valleys and rough hills.

How much distance can desert-seas call
up to divide what will always be a tomorrow
of having a grandchild approach its landfall?

I won't be there and don't expect to be on the roll
of those you will be told will *unconditionally love you*.
I hear across the valleys and gnarled hills.

If memories *are* passed along strings of cells
as well as by word of mouth, then I hope you might follow,
for I can't follow, grandchild, as you near landfall.

There's no complaint in this, and I avow
no rights at all, but I love water and all that grows,
and I hear across the valleys and gnarled hills
of a grandchild approaching its landfall.

## FOR MY CHILDREN

Photos don't tell me anything I can really know
and as I recall those *special* moments with each child
they seem to be those in which their *sense of things* grew.

I don't understand the incidents and events that grow
into the adults they have become, that complement a 'social attitude',
photos don't tell me anything I can really know.

It may be different for others, but for me it's the *window*
they moved on past and not images snapped and framed
that show instances in which their *sense of things* grew.

I miss my kids with whom the bond was broken, who
won't come on bush walks or throw ball or watch a bird feed,
photos don't tell me anything I can really know.

But one *is* still 'at home' and searching eucalypts for the glow
of *new arrivals,* for the season's shift as the sun is shifted,
and searches for words to express a *sense of how things* grow.

My children, I miss you, but don't call you from your tomorrows,
don't call you to appear in photos that are self-contained,
as photos don't tell me anything I can really know
though I wonder if for you they make a *sense of things* grow.

## ALL I'VE BREATHED IN

All the things that I've breathed in
have left their marks on my lungs,
those residues and calling cards within.

The 'I' in this might be the 'we' of a position
statement, an expression of the highly strung
*ala* all the things that I've breathed in.

Do you want to share the inhalations:
dusts of asbestos, red lead, powdered ilmenite grunge?
Those residues and calling cards within.

Or how about the fumes of tobacco and polyurethane,
or just plain old car exhaust – the city's aqualung?
All the things that I've breathed in.

And the accrual of vapours that were *odours* run
past the olfactory epithelium, wrung
to add to those residues and calling cards therein.

We might – if I are 'we' — rejoice in the inhalations
of perfumes (petrochemicals) and country air (agrichemicals)... *floating...?*
       All the things that I've breathed in
       those residues and calling cards within.

## OF FEDERATION FREE CLASSICAL ARCHITECTURE AND TREE DELETION

Little is said now of the tall trees cut down for the 'eco carpark'
solar panels in Northam, deep-rooted histories of organic architecture,
the disturbed clouds coming in fast over the river making day dark.

But remember over the far side of the shopping centre their crowns mark
an absence still, spectres of differing altitudes, something to assure,
though little is said now of the tall trees cut down for the 'eco carpark'.

A dozen species of bird returned to nest across the year but baulk
mid-air and circle away, rerouting memories, semantic drift, nothing to claw
back disturbed clouds coming in fast over the river making day dark.

But the Federation Free Classical with 'grand Italianate style façade'
    architectonic
preservation heritage conservation Grade 1 listed Town Hall building
    perseveres
though little is said now of the tall trees cut down for the 'eco carpark'.

Each 'rendered pilaster and pediment' — those arches and triangles stark
out of walls – 'pillars' of bold decoration evince form & function, *on the register*
reflections of disturbed clouds coming in fast over the river making day dark.

I am here, bothered by the angles of atmospherics, where a building remarks
as its utilities are plastered over, and the cold front staunches, reapplies
    pressure
to the trauma where tall trees were cut down for an 'eco carpark',
its disturbed clouds coming in fast over the river making day dark.

## THE FROGS


In Bird Gully vibrating and popping down into the valley-
groove, frog-calls toad-calls the pulse-rush sonars night –
crawling toadlet and pobblebonk repartee.

It's easy enough to tune out, lapse, harder to free
the earhorn to *listen* through a quelling of *the silent* –
in Bird Gully vibrating and popping down into the valley.

We've measured our presence by revegetating the leys,
we've listened with intervals and gaps hoping sound will activate
crawling toadlet and pobblebonk repartee.

The skin of our eardrums is played with grey
tones of emergence in the mostly full moon's callout –
in Bird Gully vibrating and popping down into the valley.

We are a paracosm of frogs calling defiantly
and hungrily and lustily and matter-of-factly – *imprint* –
crawling toadlet and pobblebonk repartee.

But the machine doesn't feel a frog's skin-intensity
when it hacks a way through dried surface to wet substrate –
indifferent to Bird Gully vibrating and popping with valley-
crawling toadlet and pobblebonk repartee.

## SCARLET RUNNER RHAPSODIC VILLANELLE [A VARIATION]


We wait for the storm, constraining our moods,
those unnameable clouds' inspissation over the hills
while in the darkening valley Scarlet Runner buds.

We have always used 'the weather' to shape our forms,
extracting plasma in our star-gazing parallax seasonals,
so we wait for the storm, constraining our moods.

As kids we skirted the dry places and followed
tendrils of 'Running Postman' as it delivered redwax seals,
while in the darkening valley Scarlet Runner buds.

And while such a cold-low plant will warm in its seed-memory of flame,
auguries of cellulose and sap, linalool and ocimene, pigment-wink *survival*,
and so we wait for the storm, restraining our moods.

All these plant connotations of behaviour and words,
all the reforms and plots of restoration held prostrate as squalls
entangle the darkening valley and Scarlet Runner blooms.

These snaps of insight these visages knowing how to reform
*and* attract, to defy and not deify narratives of quietus and Fall;
we wait for the storm, constraining our moods,
while in the darkening valley scarlet runner broods.

## BRIMSTONE

All the sulphur of experiments and gardens of explosions and *purifications*,
the Golden Splash Tooth the *subceracea* light of the shades and the damp
and the sun's show-through a mimicry of light and shadow-skin.

Sun's action is beneath away from its eye as under and under the canopy the fallen
wood rotting trees offer conditions and protection, the fungus grows as the gleam of a lamp,
unto the sulphur of experiments and gardens of explosions and purifications.

For the extraction the greed for the element of star formation
for contradictions in the elemental body's desire for a soothing burn a universal stamp?
And the sun's show-through a mimicry of light and shadow-skin.

Such inversions such cravings to make the chemistry of animation,
and to find these sulphury residues on wood piled in a dry place at a stable temp,
all the sulphur of experiments and gardens of explosions and purifications.

The hydrogen sulphide gas the sulphuric acid the fossil fuel by-product variations on brimstone:
and all around in every seam and crack across every surface the wattle pollen encamps;
and the sun's show-through a mimicry of light and shadow-skin.

For pollen is yellowtime is the sulphured light we sweep to horizons,
the golden splash tooth meteorite heatshield in darkness reminds us, too, and ignites a swamp;
all the sulphur of experiments and gardens of explosions and purifications,
and the sun's show-through the mimicry of light and shadow-skin.

## SILVER

*for Tracy*

Precious and transitional the cloud shifts the hills
into mirror response to erosion and stone and trees,
a family of shufflewings are conductive and celestial.

I pause to watch them work a high place – the pinnacle
of the tallest and oldest and most tangled tree at peak of valley,
precious and transitional the cloudbase shifts the hills.

I pause not to mine or extract but to let the periodic table
count its way through the years, to hesitate before the free
family of shufflewings so conductive and celestial.

Those stable isotopes that gleam of the uncaptured metal,
unreactive to air, but vulnerable to salt's eating away,
precious and transitional the cloudbase shifts the hills.

But nothing will tarnish what we have, what we will
share together or apart, involved in each other's day,
that family of shufflewings so conductive and celestial.

A catalyst for each other, a photography that entails
arm in arm without costing the animals – gelatine-free;
precious and transitional the cloud shifts the hills
as a family of shufflewings are conductive and celestial.

## YELLOW-BILLED SPOONBILL AWARENESS

As precise as a sifting stirring and arcing of submerged beak
the yellow-billed spoonbill is more than a GPS,
what it senses is assumed to be food but touch can speak.

The wader troubles crustaceans and larvae who forsake
their rapid development in sediment and substrates grazers,
as precise as a sifting stirring and arcing of angled beak.

Small eyes watch us watching them as bill works as beak
not billhook though capitalists might equate as bill of fare but not
    bill of rights?
What it senses is assumed to be food but touch can *speak*.

How does the flooded gum canopy work leaves and light to make
a harvest of life – a zone of gathering of locating and 'success'?
As precise as a sifting stirring and arcing of submerged beak.

The ingredients of the hurt river is a swelling to its peak
before breaking its banks, a riffle a downrush into silt of lotic species;
what it senses is assumed to be food but touch can *speak*.

And we read in our eyes its eyes making scare quotes of residues and freak
leakages and humdrum contaminants, parsing nekton and an upsurge
    of benthos
as precise as a sifting stirring and arcing of submerged beak –
what it senses is assumed to be food but touch *can* speak.

## FROLIC

To see a loved one emergent among birds
the flock of parrots the nesting weebills the redcaps
is to frolic as if all life has broken free of the grid.

Against extinguishment we are lured
into a sudden intensity of sap to blood, blood to sap,
to see a loved one emergent among birds.

In his shaded eyes to see flight-cured
sunlight release its rare sightings to more than a stopgap
is to frolic as if all life has broken free of the grid.

Maybe you had to feel the shift of media politics to one based
in re-tunings and refrains, escaping anthropocene relapse,
to see a loved one emergent among birds.

The bird reached but left alone is the person turned
to embrace an orchid's unfurling its flower-shape,
is to frolic as if all life has broken free of the grid.

What is cultivated in the moment is procured
in memory – witness the curvets over each synapse!
To see a loved one emergent among birds
and frolic as if all life has broken free of the grid.

## BLUE HERON ON RAIL BRIDGE OVER AVON NEAR NORTHAM

*for Tim K.*


Quick see blue heron land almost lightly on the railway bridge,
bright blue resident stand out surveying fast water below,
heavy viewfinder scissor beak to translate larvae's language.

There is no train in sight so blue heron counts minims offstage –
swoops down, decisive, to stalk slowly through reflection's shadow –
quick see blue heron launch almost lightly off the railway bridge.

Quick smart elusive while slow cautious and intricate footage,
to stir air and the waters quickly degraded with farm flow,
heavy viewfinder scissor beak to translate minnow's language.

Release pesticides and treat herbicides breezily – pillage
to make blue heron stalk grace grossly out-stepping its sorrow,
quick see blue heron land almost lightly on the railway bridge.

Brute force traverses river crossings for sound effects – poise, edge
to take hold over damage claims and the train's hope to outgrow
doubt cast – blue heron lands almost lightly on the railway bridge.

Quick see blue heron land almost lightly on the railway bridge,
heavy viewfinder scissor beak to translate minnow's language.
Quick see blue heron launch almost lightly off the railway bridge,
heavy viewfinder scissor beak to upset larvae's language.

## MAGPIE LARKS NESTING BY THE RIVER IN NORTHAM

How perfect can the perfect structure be the perfect nest
in the limb over the path in the limb reaching out to the river,
the mudlark's architecture and construction is redressed?

For though all such structures are made by mudlarks in palimpsest
they are made in the image of now of how things are,
perfect as a perfect structure can be the perfect nest.

The male waiting on eggs as the female flies in from the quickest
of feedings, nudging him out and checking things are as they were,
the mudlark's architecture and construction is redressed.

How to perfect the already perfect hut roofed at its base at rest,
an inversion of the world we've constructed as idea of shelter,
perfect as a perfect structure can be the perfect nest.

So opened to the elements open to a metaphysics to the best
and worst of a belled-sky and the surveillance of aerial predators,
the mudlark's architecture and construction is redressed.

And yet the body is a roof is a room is panopticon *ingressed*,
and the testament of building shapes release and chimes departures;
how perfect can the perfect structure be the perfect nest
the mudlark's architecture and construction is redressed.

## EXTINGUISHMENT

'Queensland extinguishes native title over Indigenous land to make way for Adani coalmine – Palaszczuk government did not announce decision Wangan and Jagalingou people say makes them trespassers on their own land'

*The Guardian*, 31st August, 2019


*As* Theia impacted Gaia to water our residence
*is not* as the coal mine is to the biosphere –
the 'left' performs fascism to extinguish land rights.

Not *that* many pay packets or flicks of a switch
or recharging of devices will come before the last fires,
though Theia impacted Gaia to water our residence.

All the words for origins, all the journeys and treks
down to the present – the elision of histories to pyres,
the 'left' performs fascism to extinguish land rights.

Whatever our manners of eternity, surely evidence
of some form of earthly dwelling seems core,
though Theia impacted Gaia to water our residence?

And in the commerce of this *new colonialism* you get that sense
that *old colonialism* is firing up its kilns and boilers,
the 'left' performs fascism to extinguish land rights.

Let's stand with the people who know the essence
of the soil and what goes deep, who know the spoilers –
as Theia impacted Gaia to water our residence,
the 'left' performs fascism to extinguish land rights.

## CHURCH AS 'DEVELOPER'

on the Anglican Church's Attempt to Push Through the Environmentally
Catastrophic Stoneville North Development Proposal / Plan

You baptised me you confirmed me
you took my childhood twenty-cent donations,
and you ravage bushland from the sacristy.

The act of possession is a toxic liturgy
and each lesson peeled-off is a dead-end lesson,
you baptised me you confirmed me.

You say it's regretful that such angry
people protest at your house of worship – sin bin –
and you ravage bushland from the sacristy.

In league with the free-market economy
what is a honeyeater what is a quenda what is a scorpion?
You baptised me you confirmed me.

The incorporating of the holy –
denomination, congregation, episcopal nominations –
and you ravage bushland from the sacristy.

Though I left you because of your hunger for money,
I can't shake the dirt of that via some media con –
you baptised me you confirmed me
and you ravage bushland from the sacristy.

## THE STORM THAT WON'T BREAK

Planting a drought garden seems absurd
especially when the ground can't be broken,
and a storm refusing to break is a final word.

Calling on a store of old heirloom seeds (not a hoard),
to hope some will still germinate and be outspoken –
planting a drought garden seems absurd.

As officials fail to act as things unfold
then act as if they were acting all along and without hesitation,
we are sold a storm breaking its word,

When these greens break through into world,
joining under with over and making miraculous transpiration,
planting a drought garden might seem less absurd.

We travel the length and breadth, we drop food
on doorsteps and see THANKS against window panes,
and remember the storm refusing to break its word.

But maybe that's desire and wish-fulfilment and mutual aid
all sprouting to make light underground in drought conditions;
planting a drought garden seems absurd
but a storm refusing to break is not the final word.

## VILLANELLE OF FIRE

On a hot night lying on top of the sheets
watching lightning flashes without rain,
fire could arrive so fast we'd barely be able to rise.

These are the conditions of crisis,
a crisis we make by increments – *portions* –
on a hot night lying on top of the sheets.

In declaring war on fire, governments
distract from their 'growth!' and 'development' refrains,
fire could arrive so fast we'd barely be able to rise.

Some people will have a chance to evacuate, others
will be led to safety, and some will burn,
on a hot night lying on top of the sheets.

Will these containment lines hold back the *climate*-deniers,
the fire in its cauldron, its search for lost oxygen?
Fire could arrive so fast we'd barely be able to rise.

We are all 'in this together', watching smoke-dead skies,
hearing billions of animals die in coaled undertones –
on a hot night lying on top of the sheets
fire could arrive so fast we'd barely be able to rise.

## EMPATHY

I have seen both brimstone moths and brimstone butterflies
in northern climes even as those zones were altering fast –
an almost pandemic of breath, then no breath whatever its course.

The patterning of dust and hairs and colour, the actions of dicots
and monocots together, the roadside verge the field edge the chalk the karst
I have seen both brimstone moths and brimstone butterflies.

A leaf lifts in a hot wind that could be the sign given, or a mimic's
co-ordination – either way, a sensitive response seems prudent –
an almost pandemic of breath, then no breath whatever its course.

Many years ago I was sent a photo of winter mist of cross-season mists
from a poet-friend in Wuhan, now I search it out but can't find the past.
I have seen sulphur up on the Peak in Hong Kong in the wings of its
    butterflies.

I have seen sulphur in wings of butterflies angling up rockfaces
at Jam Tree Gully, and sulphur in wings on Reunion and in
    American forests,
an almost pandemic of breath, then no breath whatever its course.

And as the virus flits from breath to breath, as it twists
its way into people's lives and afterlives all correlations spread *and* shift;
I have seen both brimstone moths and brimstone butterflies –
an almost pandemic of breath, then no breath whatever its course.

JOHN KINSELLA's most recent volumes of poetry are *Insomnia* (Picador, 2019), *Tangling with the Epic* (with Kwames Dawes, Peepal Tree, 2019) and *Drowning in Wheat: Selected Poems 1980-2015* (Picador, 2016). His most recent books with Arc Publications are *The Wound* (2019), *Samson Agonistes* (2018), *Comus: A Dialogic Mask* (2008) and *America (A Poem)* (2005) . His volumes of stories include *In the Shade of the Shady Tree* (Ohio University Press, 2012), *Crow's Breath* (Transit Lounge, 2015) and *Old Growth* (Transit Lounge, 2017). His volumes of criticism include *Activist Poetics: Anarchy in the Avon Valley* (Liverpool University Press, 2010) and *Polysituatedness* (Manchester University Press, 2017).

He is a Fellow of Churchill College, Cambridge University, and Professor of Literature and Environment at Curtin University, but most relevantly he is an anarchist vegan pacifist of over thirty-five years and has spent his life resisting fascism. He believes poetry is one of the most effective activist modes of expression and resistance we have.

John Kinsella wishes always to acknowledge the traditional and custodial owners of the land he comes from – the Ballardong Noongar people, the Whadjuk Noongar people, and the Yamaji people.